This book belongs to

_____

_____

and I am finding out
about the Bible

Published by Candle Books
an imprint of
Lion Hudson plc
Wilkinson House, Jordan Hill Road,
Oxford OX2 8DR, England
www.lionhudson.com/candle

ISBN 978 1 78128 104 8
e-ISBN 978 1 78128 133 8

First edition 2014

A catalogue record for this book is available
from the British Library

Printed and bound in China,
February 2014, LH06

Would you like to know
The Bible?

by Tim Dowley
Illustrated by Eira Reeves

There are lots of books in the world…

but the Bible is a very special book.

It's different from all the other books…

because it tells us about God.

The Bible tells us
how we can know God…

and become his friend.

And the Bible tells us how
God wants us to live.

The Bible is a book full of stories
about God and his people.

The Bible is in two parts
– the Old Testament...

and the New Testament.

Each part of the Bible is made of lots of shorter books joined together.
There are 39 books in the Old Testament…

Part 1

and 27 books in the New Testament.

Part 2

The Old Testament is about the people of God.

It tells us what happened
to them.

The New Testament is about
God's son, Jesus.
He is the most important person
who has lived.

The New Testament explains how we can become God's friends.

Both parts of
the Bible tell us
about how
God loves us…

and wants us to love him in return.

People all over the world
read the Bible...

and learn about God's love.

Here is a prayer you can use
when you read your Bible:

Lord Jesus, please help me learn
about you when I read my Bible.
Amen

Sometimes we need help
to understand the Bible.

You can ask someone older to help.

And you can read books
of Bible stories.